CW00508064

Table of Contents

TESTIMONIALS

These beautiful women of God were part of the very first 'in person' course that I ran. Now the course is available in book form so everyone can access it, complemented by optional audio for daily breath awareness, breath prayers and meditation.

I have just completed this very useful course and gained so much. I have been re-charged and re-energised into habits of quiet and meditation. Guided to scriptures, encouraged to use all the senses and to turn my mind onto appreciation and gratitude for all He gives us. I want to abide more, to be still more and to take in all He has created for our pleasure. I know how to breathe to my advantage, using scripture at the same time. I have picked up new tools to use when I am working with others, because I have experienced them. Our leader has a real passion, she led us gently with a knowledge of her subject. MOST BENEFICIAL!

Annie S (Counsellor)

The last couple of years have been hard, especially where my thoughts are concerned. I have struggled to renew my mind and take my thoughts captive. I knew I needed help with this as I was getting depressed worrying about it. Kerry's well-being course came just at the right time for me. It has helped me to still my mind with God's word and helped me to silence the other voices and enter into deep rest with our Father. I highly recommend, I feel so much lighter.

Liza L

Kerry is a beautiful soul. After every session I always felt like I had been bathed in peace and tranquillity. Brilliant way to jump off the treadmill of life for a while.

Kathrine W

From the moment I stepped into the sessions of the 'Eden Well-being' I felt change and movement in my life. My daughter who was struggling with terrible anxiety and fear asked if she could come along with me. Kerry welcomed her with open arms and the difference after just one afternoon amongst prayer and relaxation was astonishing. My daughter said as she walked outside afterwards the whole world seemed brighter and clearer. She has since made life changing steps to a brighter future; she is full of peacefulness instead of fear. The course for myself made me feel calmer, relaxed and to remember how eternally grateful I am for our beautiful world we've been given from our Lord. I would highly recommend this course if you are struggling in anyway and for your eyes to be wide open to our Father.

Lorraine T

The well-being course was welcoming, filled with warmth, calm, peace and serenity. The setting was truly amazing filled with compassion, fellowship and above all the unity in love for the Lord. Meditation and scriptures were very well complemented and well researched. The entire course provided a much more thoughtful and peaceful mind to take home.

Julie D

INTRODUCTION

My first introduction to church was in the run up to my marriage to James in 2001.

If we were going to get married in a church and have children in the future, after a discussion with my husband to be, we decided we would begin to attend the services at Sandon Church in Staffordshire.

Our first-born son Jacob arrived in 2002 and Sophie Mae in 2006.

Everything in my life was perfect, except I sensed something was missing that nothing else could fill. I had been struggling with depression and anxiety, feeling fearful of the world my children were growing up in and worrying about the future.

In 2013 after having a short time out of church, a friend invited me on an Alpha course and I began to understand what it meant to have a relationship with The Trinity; Father God, Jesus Son of God and The Holy Spirit.

It really was a lightbulb moment for me. For the first time I understood personally how God had sent His Son into the world to reconcile me back to Himself. How Jesus died on the cross to take all my sins so that I could be forgiven and by accepting Him as my Lord and Saviour I would receive eternal life and have The Holy Spirit live within me.

I wanted to receive everything that God had for me and serve him with all my heart.

I threw myself into every bit of learning I could and after seeking the Lord of what gifts he wanted to develop through me and use for his glory he led me to Christian Relaxation and Meditation. My heart has always been to help other people not only to be well, but to thrive in their journey also with the Lord.

I had a number of Christian and Non-Christian friends who were going through some difficult times and needed extra support and were searching for peace in the world. Some had found peace for a short time, but then found themselves back in the same place struggling or worse still. As a Christian we have to be careful what we involve ourselves in and open ourselves up to because of where the practice is rooted.

As I prayed about it, a sister in Christ confirmed what I was hearing from the Lord, and so in 2017 I started a small group in my lounge 'Christian Relaxation and Meditation'.

It went so well the group began to grow, and I began to run it as a course at the church I was attending several times a year.

During the pandemic 2020-2021 I took the course online and during 2022 I ran two wellbeing courses at a friend's farm in the countryside.

I realised during this time that I needed to go deeper with some teachings as many people were still struggling and to give them the tools to use in between and after following the course.

As the last wellbeing course ended for the year, I felt the Lord leading me to do some studying so that I would be better equipped for what He had planned for me to do going forwards.

I took two accredited courses, Cognitive Behavioural Therapy 'CBT' and Mindfulness based Cognitive Therapy 'MBCT'.

Cognitive behavioural therapy (CBT) is a talking therapy that can help you manage your problems by changing the way you think and behave. It's most commonly used to treat anxiety and depression, but can be useful for other mental and physical health problems. Mindfulness or being mindful works really well with CBT by focusing awareness on the present moment as a gift from God rather than dwelling on thoughts past or future.

As I went along with the courses, I could see that when we start to look at values, identity and truth as a foundation in our lives, if it is built on anything other than a solid foundation it has the potential to fall apart. As with the wise and foolish builders in Matthew 7:24-27.

When the word of God is brought to the centre of all we do, change is ultimately transformational.

CHRISTIAN MEDITATION

There are significant differences in both the intention and practice of secular, Eastern and Christian forms of meditation. Christian meditation is a classical spiritual discipline that is rooted deeply in the bible and in ancient Christian practice. The intention of filling the mind with thoughts of God and with scripture and being transformed by the renewal of your mind and into the likeness of Christ.

Joshua 1.8

'This Book of the Law shall not depart from your mouth, but you shall meditate on it day and night, so that you may be careful to do according to all that is written in it. For then you will make your way prosperous, and then you will have good success'.

Psalm 1.1-3

'Blessed is the man who walks not in the counsel of the wicked, nor stands in the way of sinners, nor sits in the seat of scoffers; but his delight is in the law of the Lord, and on his law he meditates day and night. He is like a tree planted by streams of water that yield its fruit in its season, and its leaf does not wither. In all that he does, he prospers'.

Romans 12.2

'Do not be conformed to this world, but be transformed by the renewal of your mind, that by testing you may discern what is the will of God, what is good and acceptable and perfect'.

If you are new to meditating you may be wondering if it's difficult to attain. The reality is this, if you know how to worry then you know how to meditate!

The idea is that we can meditate on scripture whilst we walk, do the shopping, in the middle of the night, as well as to sit and relax. We can be in the middle of a crowded, noisy, potentially stressful situation but if you know how to meditate on God's word you can know the peace of God literally anywhere.

EDEN

God's originally designed atmosphere for man to flourish was Eden - The Garden of Eden.

The name Eden is of Hebrew origin meaning "place of pleasure". The perfect garden in which Adam and Eve were placed at the Creation.

WELL-BEING

Well-being is a combination of whole life wellness - Body, Mind and Spirit. The biblical concept of wellness is captured in the Hebrew word "Shalom" meaning peace, harmony, wholeness and completeness.

I have put this Christian well-being course together using some of what I learnt within CBT/MBCT ultimately led by God. The first course began Sept 2023 alongside enrolling on 'Leadership' college with church.

We can learn to walk in all God has given us through the death and resurrection of His Son Jesus and the power of The Holy Spirit if we study the Bible and practise His presence on a daily basis.

In addition to this wellbeing book, I have an audio which includes breath awareness, breath prayers and a meditation which applies to the teaching. Where you meditate is up to you, but combined with the relaxation techniques it is essential you are in a place where you can close your eyes and take some time out to relax which I recommend for 10-20 minutes 5 out of 7 days.

I would also encourage you to get into the habit of meditating on God's word, during your bible study if the Holy Spirit highlights a piece of scripture, if you want to meditate on a promise or to understand what God is saying to you personally.

This course is most beneficial as a six-week course. Study and practice one session per week.

SESSION ONE - Introduction to BEING MINDFUL, BREATH PRAYERS, MEDITATION

Being mindful is about being in the moment and something we should be practising to incorporate in our life. As we go through the sessions, I will give you ideas on how you can learn to be more mindful each and every day.

The benefits of being mindful

* Decreases stress, depression, anxiety and overwhelm.

* Improves general health.

* Improves memory, concentration and focus.

* Lessons emotional reactivity.

* Improves quality of life and wellbeing.

I believe as a Christian being mindful each day allows us to connect with the Holy Spirit at a deeper level by slowing our minds down from running at 100mph and taking time to connect with the here and now and what he is trying to show and communicate to us. The bible consistently encourages us to exercise disciplined attentiveness to our minds and hearts, to set aside our attachment to ourselves, and to live in God's moment to moment provision. By being present and attentive, spending time with God we begin to take in the beauty that surrounds us. We naturally begin to show gratitude to God for the small things as well as the big things in our lives and ultimately experience life together with God.

In this first session I want to spend some time practising being mindful each day, using breath awareness, breath prayers and Meditation. However, we start every session with a teaching or reading and in this first session we consider what it means to 'Abide in Christ Jesus'.

Read **The True Vine** - John 15:1-17

Abiding in Jesus starts with stillness. So right now, pause, take a deep breath, anything concerning you give it over to God through His son Jesus.

To abide is to live, continue or remain. To abide in Jesus is to live in Him or remain in Him.

To abide in Jesus, we must begin by...

Believing that He is God's son.

1 John 4:15 'Whoever confesses that Jesus is the son of God, God abides in him, and he in God'.

Receiving Him as Lord and saviour.

John 1:12 'But to all who did receive Him, who believed in His name, he gave the right to become children of God'.

Doing what God says.

1 John 3:24 'Whoever keeps these commandments abides in God and God in Him'.

Continuing to believe the gospel.

1 John 2:24 'Let what you heard from the beginning abide in you, if what you heard from the beginning abides in you, then you too will abide in the son and the father'.

Relating in love to the community of believers.

John 15:12 'This is my commandment that you love one another as I have loved you'.

Many people try to be good, honest people who do what is right. But Jesus says that the only way to live a truly good life is to stay close to Him, to abide in Him. Just like branches attached to the vine. Apart from Jesus our efforts are unfruitful.

Receive the nourishment and life offered by Jesus, the vine.

BREATH AWARENESS

We have been breathing subconsciously all of our lives, it's perhaps not something we often think about whether we are breathing well or not.

Most people find that they are shallow breathers, breathing into the chest. Shallow breathing limits the diaphragm's range of motion. The lowest part of the lungs does not get a full share of oxygenated air. That can make you feel short of breath or anxious.

Deep abdominal breathing encourages full oxygen exchange, that is, the beneficial trade of incoming oxygen for outgoing carbon dioxide. This deeper breathing has a calming effect on the nervous system and helps you to be relaxed and calm.

Practising breath awareness can help when you find yourself in stressful situations, it also helps you to be mindful of the present moment as a gift from God. With each breath you can call upon the name of the Lord, say the name of Jesus with each inhale and each exhale to bring your focus back to him at any given moment.

Spend 5 minutes practising this deep way of breathing. Inhale through your nose (if you are able) breathe deeply so you can feel your abdomen expand, hold for a few seconds before releasing your breath slowly through your mouth.

BREATH PRAYERS

Breath prayers are an ancient form of prayer linked to the rhythms of breathing. Rooted in scripture, breath prayers are short, mainly of one sentence.

Aligned with the rhythm of the breath, the first half is prayed while inhaling, the second half is prayed while exhaling.

Job 33.4 'The spirit of God has made me, the breath of the Almighty gives me life'.

Breathe in; (repeating the words in your mind) The spirit of God has made me.

Breathe out; The breath of the almighty gives me life.

God is in every breath that we take, the more we practise breath prayers, the more we learn to pray without ceasing.

MEDITATION

Spend some time now to centre your heart on the one who matters most, try and spend 5 minutes meditating on the following scripture.

John 14:4 'Abide in Me, and I in you'

Read again John 15:1-17

Close your eyes again, breathe deeply in through your nose and out through your mouth.

As you meditate this time, emphasise the first word, then the second word and so on until you have emphasised each word.

John 15:4 'Abide in me and I in you'.

Now spend a little time meditating on the following scripture, again using the technique of emphasising a different word each time.

Psalm 46:10 'Be still and know that I am God'.

PRAYER

Dear Heavenly Father, I thank you for your son, Jesus, who made a way for me to be reconciled back to you by His death on the cross and forgiveness of all my sins. That by accepting Him as Lord and saviour gave me the right to be called a child of God. I thank you for your word made alive to me through the power of The Holy Spirit, that it is a solid foundation for me to build my life upon. As I consider and meditate upon what it truly means for you to abide in me and I in you, I ask that you would take me on this journey to know you more. In Jesus name I pray, Amen.

MINDFULNESS ACTIONS

Practice 5 out of 7 days.

Breath Awareness

Breath Prayers - Job 33:4

Meditation - John 15:4 and Psalm 46:10

Saying grace - At least one meal a day, taking the time to prepare a healthy and nutritious meal/snack. Enjoy with a glass of water, before or afterwards.

<u>Example of Prayer</u>

"Father God, I praise you for the nourishment that you provide. Thank you for meeting my physical needs of hunger and thirst. Forgive me for taking that simple joy for granted, I ask that you would bless this food to fuel my body. I pray that I will be energised and be able to work for the glory of Your Kingdom. In Jesus name, Amen.

As you now enjoy your meal, engage your God given senses to see, smell, taste.

Savour small bites and chew thoroughly.

Note how better you feel hydrating your body with water. All good things come from God.

SESSION TWO - TAKING OUR THOUGHTS CAPTIVE

WHAT ARE THOUGHTS?

Thoughts are mental cognitions, our ideas, opinions, and beliefs about ourselves and the world around us. They include the perspectives we bring to any situation or experience that colours our point of view (for better, worse or neutral).

An example of a long-lived thought is an attitude, which develops as thoughts are repeated over and over and reinforced.

While thoughts are shaped by life experiences, genetics, and education, they are generally under conscious control. In other words, if you are aware of your thoughts and attitudes, you can choose to change them.

2 Corinthians 10:5 tells us to take our thoughts captive, it is an essential part of emotional, physical and spiritual wellbeing.

'We destroy arguments and every lofty opinion raised against the knowledge of God, and take every thought captive to obey Christ'.

Taking your thoughts captive simply means gaining control over what you think about yourself and life.

With good reason, as every day we all have thousands of thoughts run through our mind. Left unexamined, our thoughts can get out of control that leads to negative and unhealthy emotions and feelings.

WE ARE NOT OUR THOUGHTS

This is especially important to remember if the thoughts are troublesome and have a negative impact on your well-being.

As you take a thought captive you then ask yourself the following questions...

1. Does this thought line up with what I believe in accordance with the word of God?

2. Is this way of thinking bringing glory to God or bringing me closer in my relationship with Him?

3. Are these thoughts producing more faith and trust in God, or am I choosing worry and fear?

When you have a thought, as you take that thought captive you can judge if that thought is good or bad, true or false based on the word of God.

WHAT ARE EMOTIONS/FEELINGS?

Without going deep into psychology, a short explanation would be that emotions come first, as those chemicals go to work in your body then come the feelings.

The mood then develops from a combination of feelings.

THOUGHTS LEAD TO EMOTIONS...

Each emotion and then feeling we have starts with a thought, when we recognise that we can begin to understand why we feel the way we do and why it is important to take our thoughts captive as the word of God instructs us.

(Some examples)

THOUGHTS	EMOTIONS/FEELINGS
Hopelessness and regret	Sadness/depression
Worry	Anxiety
Gratitude	Joy
God is in control	Hope

In this exercise I want you to consider the emotions/feelings that you have had recently.

Position the emotion/feeling under the Healthy and Unhealthy column (see some of my examples and then add your own).

HEALTHY EMOTION	UNHEALTHY EMOTION
Calm	Guilt
Fulfilment	Jealousy

There may be a couple of emotions that could possibly fall into either healthy or unhealthy for example.

Fear

Proverbs 1:7 'The fear of the Lord is the beginning of knowledge, but fools despise wisdom and instruction'.

Honour and respect of God, to live in awe of His power, and to obey His word.

Anger

Mark 3:5 'And he looked around at them with anger, grieved at their hardness of heart' (Jesus displayed righteous anger).

Jesus expressed His anger by correcting a problem.

PAYING ATTENTION

In this next exercise as you consider some emotions and feelings that you have experienced recently, are you able to trace it back to what you have been thinking about?

As you do this you can begin to recognise any unhealthy or healthy thinking patterns and what effect it may be having on your emotions and then your feelings.

EMOTIONS/FEELINGS   **THOUGHTS**

So, we can now begin to see a connection between what we are thinking about and the effect on our emotions, feelings and overall well-being. We now understand why God instructs us to take our thoughts captive.

Romans 12.2

'Do not be conformed to this world, but be transformed by the renewal of your mind, that by testing you may discern what is the will of God, what is good and acceptable and perfect'.

Hebrews 4:12

For the word of God is living and active, sharper than any two-edged sword piercing to the division of soul and of the spirit, of joints and of marrow, and discerning the thoughts and intentions of the heart'.

John 8:32 'Then you will know the truth, and the truth will set you free'.

When you dwell on the truth in God's word - peace will come.

FORMING A PLAN (to take thoughts captive)

Recognising the thoughts before they begin to spiral out of control. Begin to journal any repetitive thought patterns, and ask yourself, does it line up with the word of God?

Is it true or is it a lie?

Whatever the issue, there is a solution in God's word, most of us are visual learners and need reminders to choose the truth. Write your verse, on a small card or sticky note, take it with you in your pocket or put it somewhere you will see it throughout the day. Look at it, memorise it, and meditate upon it. Speak out the verse as many times as you need to in order to begin to take your thoughts captive and know the truth.

SOME EXAMPLES OF TAKING THOUGHTS CAPTIVE (make it personal)

THOUGHT: I can't do it, I'm no good.

GOD'S WORD: Philippians 4:13 'I can do all things through him who strengthens me'.

THOUGHT: I am afraid, I don't feel in control.

GOD'S WORD: 2 Timothy 1:7 'For God gave us a spirit not of fear but of power, and love and self-control'.

THOUGHT: I don't like what I see when I look into the mirror.

GOD'S WORD: Psalm 139:14 'I praise you for I am fearfully and wonderfully made'.

THOUGHT: I'm not a nice person, I've done some terrible things.

GOD'S WORD: 2 Corinthians 5:17 'Therefore if anyone is in Christ, he is a new creation. The old has passed away, behold the new has come'.

Romans 8:1 'There is therefore now no condemnation for those who are in Christ Jesus'.

THOUGHT: I just feel so anxious and worried.

GOD'S WORD: Philippians 4:6-7 'do not be anxious about anything, but in everything by prayer and supplication with thanksgiving let your requests be made known to God. And the peace of God, which surpasses all understanding will guard your hearts and minds in Christ Jesus.

THOUGHT: I'm not sure that I'm saved.

GOD'S WORD: John 10:28 'I give them eternal life, and they will never perish, and no one is able to snatch them out of the Father's hand'.

Romans 10:9 'because, if you confess with your mouth that Jesus is Lord and believe in your heart that God raised Him from the dead, you will be saved'.

USE THIS SPACE TO WRITE THE THOUGHTS YOU HAVE TAKEN CAPTIVE (and replace with God's word).

The good news is this, with practice you can form new, healthy brain patterns when you take your thoughts captive with God's word.

BREATH AWARENESS

Place both hands on your upper abdomen. Breathing in deeply and slowly through your nose (if you are able), the aim is to feel your hands on your abdomen rise. Hold for a few seconds and then breathe out steadily through your mouth.

Shallow breathing happens in your chest, which is part of the fight or flight system. Deep diaphragmatic breathing happens in your stomach and calms the nervous system.

Build up the time in which you practise this way of breathing 'deeply' it will eventually become your new normal.

The breath is symbolic of the gift of life that God has given you.

Job 33:4

'The spirit of God has made me, the breath of the Almighty gives me life'.

BREATH PRAYERS

Taken from John 8:32 'and you will know the truth and the truth will set you free'.

Breathe in; and you will know the truth.

Breathe out; and the truth will set you free.

MEDITATION

Philippians 4:8-9 (ESV)

Finally, brothers, whatever is true, whatever is honourable, whatever is just, whatever is pure, whatever is lovely, whatever is commendable, if there is any excellence, if there is anything worthy of praise, think about these things. What you have learned and received and heard and seen in me - practise these things, and the God of peace will be with you.

As you look at this scripture is there a word that stands out to you? Is it true, honourable, just, pure, lovely, commendable, of excellence or worthy of praise?

Make a note of which word speaks to you and how you need to focus your current thoughts at the moment.

Spend some time now meditating on the following...

Lord, turn my thoughts to what is (insert your word).

Colossians 1:16-17 'For by him all things were created, in heaven and on earth, visible and invisible, whether thrones or dominions or rulers or authorities - all things were created through him and for him. And he is before all things, and in him all things hold together'.

PRAYER

Dear Heavenly Father, you created all things, in heaven and on earth, both visible and invisible. And, not only did you make everything, but you are also holding all things together through your very being, nothing that I deal with including any troublesome thoughts are outside of your domain. I may not understand my own mind at times, God, but you do and I trust you are more than able to redeem the thoughts in my head. I thank you that Jesus experienced similar emotions and feelings to me, that He was a perfect role model to me and how I should think and conduct my life. I thank you for your word Father, that there is a solution to every problem I face and a truth to every lie I have listened to or believed. I pray by the power of your Holy Spirit that you will help me to take my thoughts captive quickly and recognise any untruths or troublesome thoughts at the root and replace it with your word which has final authority. I ask that you would help me to think about those things that are honourable, whatever is just, whatever is pure, whatever is lovely, whatever is commendable, if there is anything of excellence, if there is anything worthy of praise, that you would help me to think of such things. That I will be able to put into practice all that I have learnt, and received, and heard and seen in you. That your peace shall be with me. Amen.

MINDFULNESS ACTIONS

Practice 5 out of 7 days.

Breath Awareness

Breath Prayers John 8;32

Meditate on Philippians 4:8-9

Saying grace - At least one meal a day, taking the time to prepare a healthy and nutritious meal/snack. Enjoy with a glass of water, before or afterwards.

Add this week…

Mindful walk/time outside - if you are able, I would like to encourage you to set aside time to have a mindful walk with the intention of noticing all God has created. Begin with a prayer, invite God's presence, ask the Holy Spirit to lead and guide you. As you step outside take a few moments to breathe deeply 'Job 33.4 'The spirit of God has made me, the breath of the Almighty gives me life'

Walking with intention while paying full attention to the present moment. Using your senses, sight, hearing, smell and sensations on your skin. Take time to notice the beauty in nature that is all around you, sounds of nature, smell from nature. As you do this it is an opportunity to be completely present with God, taking notice of all he has created. At the end of your walk, you may wish to spend some quiet time reflecting on God's goodness and giving thanks in prayer.

SESSION THREE - IDENTITY

It's mind blowing to think that a different version of you exists in the mind of everyone who knows you, we are not the same person to our parents, siblings, our friends and to our coworkers, neighbours etc. The person you think of as yourself exists only for you, and this is dependent sometimes on what is going on in your life and how you feel on any given day!

We tend to think of our identity as who we are as a person, or what we do as a person.

Identity exercise, this is based on how we see ourselves from a worldly perspective.

I've started with a few examples, please add your own.

I am...	**I am a...**
Honest	Wife/Husband
Loving	Carer
Sensitive	Chef

As you see from the exercise 'I am' is still largely dependent on how you feel about yourself, this has a tendency to vary based on your emotions, experiences, behaviours, upbringing or on what others have said to you or about you.

Your identity may also be based upon family, career, success and as with life when situations change you can be left feeling lost and ultimately unsure of who you are.

These statements may describe an aspect of who you are but if your true identity is not built upon a solid foundation, it won't be very secure, and going through life you may find yourself easily shaken. That is why it is vitally important to know your identity is in who Christ says you are and who you are in Him.

The world may tell you that everything that you need is already within yourself, and in a way that is true based on the fact that God knit you together in your mother's womb, however, you can only truly access what God has placed within you when you are reconciled back to God through Jesus. His identity has always been yours, could it be that God gave you your true identity at conception? (Jeremiah 1:5).

If you have accepted Jesus into your life as Lord and saviour your identity encompasses all the abundance of being a beloved child of God.

The good news is that your identity is not dependent upon what you think of yourself or what anyone else thinks of you!

Understanding your identity in God starts with taking your eyes off yourself and placing them on Him, understanding who He is, what He says about Himself, and what He says about you.

2 Corinthians 5:17

'Therefore, if anyone is in Christ, he is a new creation. The old has passed away; behold, the new has come'.

God is unchanging, He is reliable and your identity in Him is a solid foundation that cannot be shaken.

Hebrews 13:8

'Jesus Christ is the same yesterday and today, and forever'.

Galatians 2:20

'I have been crucified with Christ. It is no longer I who live, but Christ who lives in me'.

Hebrews 6:19

'We have this as a sure and steadfast anchor of the soul, a hope that enters into the inner place behind the curtain'.

God's love for us is truly unconditional, for once we have our identity in Christ, we become who we really are - Children of God, made in His image.

Genesis 1:27

'So God created man in his own image, in the image of God he created him; male and female he created them'.

This is your permanent identity, it cannot be broken, changed or taken away.

Ephesians 2:10

'For we are his workmanship, created in Christ Jesus for good works, which God prepared beforehand, that we should walk in them'.

1 Peter 2:9

'But you are a chosen race, a royal priesthood, a holy nation, a people for his own possession, that you may proclaim the excellencies of him who called you out of darkness into his marvellous light'.

So, with this in mind we can rewrite our true identity, over the next couple of weeks keep adding to the list and finding the relevant scripture.

I am...	I am a...
I am Loved (1 John 3:1)	I am a child of God (John 1:12)
I am adopted as God's child (Eph. 1:5)	I am a new creation (2 Cor 5:17)
I am forgiven (Col 3:13)	I am a member of God's household (Eph 2:19)
I am chosen (Eph 1:4)	I am a masterpiece (Eph 2:10)
I am blessed (Eph 1:3)	I am a saint (1 Cor 1:2)
I am blessed (Eph 1:3)	I am a holy temple (1 Cor 6:19)
I am in Him (1 Cor 1:30)	I am a light in the world (Matt 5:14)
I have purpose (Jeremiah 29:11)	I am a royal priesthood (1 Peter 2:9)
I am secure (2 Cor 1:22)	I am a holy nation (1 Peter 2:9)
I am set free (Gal 5:1)	
I am set apart (1 Peter 2:9)	

I am…   **I am a…**

When we have the knowledge of who he is within us that then becomes our 'true identity'. Our identity is for the sake of making known His identity.

We love because he first loved us (1 John 4:19)

We forgive because we are forgiven (Eph 4:32)

We care because he cares for us (1 Peter 5:6-7)

Take some time to think about the way your life is different now in light of who Christ is in you. Note down a few thoughts that come to mind in light of this truth.

Your identity is a gift from God, His spirit makes it a living reality over a lifetime. When you see Him face to face, you will know who He truly is, and you will fully know who you are.

1 Cor 13:12

'For now we see in a mirror dimly, but then face to face'.

Your true identity is imperishable.

BREATH AWARENESS

Spend 5-10 minutes practising this deep way of breathing. Inhale through your nose, breathe deeply so you can feel your abdomen expand, hold for a few seconds before releasing your breath slowly through your mouth.

BREATH PRAYERS

Psalm 139:13-14

'For you formed my inward parts; you knitted me together in my mother's womb. I praise you, for I am fearfully and wonderfully made. Wonderful are your works; my soul knows it very well'.

Breathe in; You created my inmost being,

Breathe out; I am fearfully and wonderfully made.

MEDITATION

His love for us is truly unconditional, for once we accept our identity in Christ, we become who we really are - children of God.

1 John 3:1

'See what kind of love the Father has given us, that we should be called children of God; and so we are. The reason why the world does not know us is that it did not know Him'.

As we meditate let's break the scripture down, repeating several times in our mind before bringing the whole scripture together.

1 John 3:1 'See what kind of love the father has given us'

What words stand out to you? Emphasise that word as you meditate now…

1 John 3:1 'See what kind of love the father has given us, that we should be called children of God; and so we are'

Do any other words stand out to you? Again, emphasise that word as you meditate now…

1 John 3:1 'See what kind of love the father has given us, that we should be called children of God; and so we are. The reason why the world does not know us is that it did not know Him'.

PRAYER

Dear Heavenly Father, may I learn to live defined by who I am in your son Jesus by the power of the Holy Spirit. Your word says that I am loved unconditionally, a new creation, forgiven, adopted, chosen, redeemed, set apart, a friend, your handiwork, seated at your right hand, hidden in you, more than a conqueror, fearfully and wonderfully made. May I live each day standing upon the truth written in your word, knowing my true identity. Amen.

Ephesians 3:14-21 - A Prayer for Spiritual Strength.

For this reason I bow my knees before the father, from whom every family in heaven and on earth is named, that according to the riches of his glory he may grant me to be strengthened with power through his spirit in my inner being, so that Christ may dwell in my heart through faith - that I, being rooted and grounded in love, may have the strength to comprehend with all the saints what is the breadth and length and height and depth, and to know the love of Christ that surpasses knowledge, that I may be filled with all the fullness of God. Now to him who is able to do far more abundantly than all I could ask or think, according to the power at work within me, to him be the glory in the church and in Christ Jesus throughout all generations, for ever and ever, Amen.

MINDFULNESS ACTIONS

Practice 5 out of 7 days.

Breath Awareness

Breath Prayers - Psalm 139: 13-14

Meditation - 1 John 3:1

Saying grace - At least one meal a day, taking the time to prepare a healthy and nutritious meal/snack. Enjoy with a glass of water, before or afterwards.

Mindful Walk or time outside - As with last week take some time to appreciate nature, God's creation.

Add this week...

Find a leaf or flower, hold it in your hand and let your attention be absorbed by it. Really look closely at the intricate detail, the colour, the shape, how it feels in your hand. Is it smooth, or rough, examine all sides and explore if it has a smell. Invite the Holy Spirit to speak to you about God's beautiful creation in this moment.

SESSION FOUR - GRATITUDE

Studies have shown that the more grateful a person is the happier they are.

When we express gratitude and receive the same, our brain is said to release dopamine and serotonin, two crucial neurotransmitters responsible for emotions that make us feel good. The more we think positive, grateful thoughts, it is claimed that, the happier and healthier we feel.

The benefits of expressing gratitude are associated with a host of mental and physical benefits. Studies have shown that feeling thankful can improve sleep, boost your mood and immunity. Gratitude can reduce depression, lesson anxiety, support heart health and bring a calm sense of well-being.

Gratitude is a positive, healthy emotion that helps us to see what's good in our lives, even through life's trials and blessings, cultivating a heart of gratitude is good for us.

Gratitude glorifies God as we praise Him and give Him thanks. By expressing gratitude, we can find joy and peace in our lives and also strengthen our relationship with God.

Psalm 138:1

'I give you thanks, O Lord, with my whole heart'.

When we really start to count our blessings and think about all that we are grateful for in our lives it reminds us of God's goodness, His unconditional everlasting love, grace and mercy.

WHAT DO WE HAVE TO BE GRATEFUL FOR?

When situations or circumstances in our lives are good or not so good, we always have so much to be grateful for. The basis of our gratitude daily should be the free gift we have been given in Christ.

God sent his only son to die in our place.

John 3:16

'For God so loved the world, that he gave his only Son, that whoever believes in him should not perish but have eternal life'.

Jesus died for us whilst we were still sinners.

Romans 5:8

'But God shows his love for us in that while we were still sinners, Christ died for us'.

Jesus' death on the cross reconciled us back to Father God.

Colossians 1:19-20

'For in him all the fullness of God was pleased to dwell, and through him to reconcile to himself all things, whether on earth or in heaven, making peace by the blood of his cross'.

We have Hope in Jesus.

Romans 8:28-30

'And we know that for those who love God all things work together for good, for those who are called according to his purpose. For those whom he foreknew he also predestined to be conformed to the image of his Son, in order that he might be the firstborn among many brothers. And those whom he predestined he also called, and those whom he called he also justified, and those whom he justified he also glorified'.

Eternal life is a free gift.

Romans 6:23

'For the wages of sin is death, but the free gift of God is eternal life in Christ Jesus our Lord'.

GRATITUDE EXERCISE

Based on who God is and what Jesus died to give you, write down at least three things you are grateful for.

Shift your focus to what you are grateful for in your life today.

It could be something big or small, it could be something as simple as waking up this morning, the air that you breathe, the birds singing in the trees, a roof over your head.

As we practise looking for things to be grateful for, it helps us to recognise what is good and what is of God.

Write down at least three more things you are grateful for today.

Whatever has come to mind, place your attention on giving thanks to God for those things.

As we practise being grateful it prevents us from taking things for granted or having a sense of entitlement.

1 Timothy 6:6

'But Godliness with contentment is of great gain. For we brought nothing into the world, and we cannot take anything out of the world'.

Gratitude deepens faith.

Psalm 136:1

'Give thanks to the Lord, for he is good, for his steadfast love endures forever'.

Being honest with ourselves do we find it easy to be grateful, or is it a struggle for us to see the good and give thanks to God in all situations and circumstances?

1 Thessalonians 5:16-18

'Rejoice always, pray without ceasing, give thanks in all circumstances; for this is the will of God in Christ Jesus for you'.

Gratitude opens our eyes to the simple beauty of ordinary days; it lets us see this day and this moment as a gift from God.

Psalm 118:24

'This is the day that the Lord has made, let us rejoice and be glad in it'.

BREATH AWARENESS

Spend 5-10 minutes practising this deep way of breathing. Inhale through your nose (if you are able) breathe deeply so you can feel your abdomen expand, hold for a few seconds before releasing your breath slowly through your mouth.

BREATH PRAYERS

Psalm 118:24 'This is the day that the Lord has made, let us rejoice and be glad in it'.

Breathe in; This is the day that the Lord has made,

Breathe out; let us rejoice and be glad in it.

MEDITATION

1 Thessalonians 5:16-18

'Rejoice always, pray without ceasing, give thanks in all circumstances; for this is the will of God in Christ Jesus for you'.

Practise breaking down the scripture as you meditate before bringing it all together.

1 Thessalonians 5:16-18

'Rejoice always, pray without ceasing…

1 Thessalonians 5:16-18

'Rejoice always, pray without ceasing, give thanks in all circumstances…

1 Thessalonians 5:16-18

'Rejoice always, pray without ceasing, give thanks in all circumstances; for this is the will of God in Christ Jesus for you'.

PRAYER

Dear Heavenly Father, when I consider all things there is always so much to be grateful for. Would you help to bring to my remembrance everything that you have done for me when I pause to count my blessings. You created this beautiful world, animals and nature for me to experience and enjoy. Thank you for sending your only son Jesus so that I could be reconciled back to you, that He would die in my place so that I could have an everlasting life which is the greatest gift of all. Thank you for the hope I have in Jesus, for life and in death, everything is taken care of by you. Thank you for the Holy spirit who lives within me to help me with every aspect of my life, leading and guiding me every day. Thank you for the gift of prayer, that I can have a relationship with you, the creator of heaven and earth. Thank You for this precious gift of life and your breath in my lungs. I will declare that this is the day that you have made Lord, I will rejoice and be glad in it. Amen.

MINDFULNESS ACTIONS

Gratitude

Start to build a list of gratefulness to God for who he is and what he died to give you. This is the foundation that our gratitude is built upon.

Each day in your journal write at least three things that you are grateful to God for on that day. Each day needs to be different to build upon your gratefulness, give thanks to God in prayer.

Practice 5 out of 7 days.

Breath Awareness

Breath Prayers - Psalm 118:24

Meditation - 1 Thessalonians 5:16-18

Saying grace - At least one meal a day, taking the time to prepare a healthy and nutritious meal/snack. Enjoy with a glass of water, before or afterwards.

Mindful walk or time outside.

SESSION FIVE - PEACE

What do you think of when you think of peace?

Maybe it is one of these scenarios…

Sitting undisturbed with a book and your favourite drink in a comfy armchair?

Lying on a beach with nothing but the sounds of the waves lapping the shore with the warmth of the sun on your body?

Spending some time in nature, enjoying the scenery and listening to bird song?

The absence of all worries and cares with everything ticked off your to do list?

Are there any other ideas of what peace looks like for you?

Very early on in my walk with the Lord, I was overcoming depression and anxiety, but as a family we were looking forward to the most wonderful holiday in Florida. I had all my hopes on this holiday and looked forward to it so much as a change from my worries at home and a place to find my peace, and calm my anxious mind. Everything about the holiday was wonderful, the weather, the experiences, being with family I felt so blessed but sadly I was really struggling with anxiety and found it very upsetting that I couldn't truly enjoy the holiday and experience the peace I was searching for. Back home a friend said to me 'you must feel better now after that lovely holiday' and my response was 'yes, it was a lovely holiday if only I could have not taken my anxious mind with me'.

The English dictionary describes the word 'Peace' as the freedom from disturbance; tranquillity or a state or period in which there is no war or a war has ended.

Most people are searching for inner peace and the world often tells us to look within for peace, that everything you need is already within, you can even find a lot of advice online on how to cultivate inner peace.

After doing an online search some of the suggestions were… Meditation, being mindful, cultivating a positive mindset, practising self-care, visualising a peaceful place, breath awareness, enjoying nature, being grateful, working on acceptance, being non-judgemental, cultivating deeper connections and the list goes on.

Most of these suggestions are good, however peace offered by the world is an empty promise and can only bring temporary comfort.

Long Term sustainable peace is not found in a place, family member, friend, hobby, time of stillness or something we can make for ourselves. Life can be tough and when struggles close in we need something more. As Christians we know that when we bring God into the centre of all we do (as we have practised in this course) it is powerful and often transformational.

According to the bible, the peace of God which transcends all understanding (the harmony and calmness of body, mind and spirit) supersedes earthly circumstances.

Nearly all the letters that Paul of the Bible wrote began with 'Grace and peace to you from God our father and the Lord Jesus Christ'. Throughout scripture we find that peace is defined as a blessing from God and harmonious with His character.

HOW CAN WE KNOW TRUE PEACE?

True peace is found only in the person Jesus Christ, everything that He died to give you is available to you through the power of the Holy Spirit.

Galatians 2:20 'I have been crucified with Christ. It is no longer I who live, but Christ who lives within me'.

Isaiah 9:6 'For to us a child is born, to us a son is given; and the government shall be upon his shoulder, and his name shall be called Wonderful Counsellor, Mighty God, Everlasting Father, Prince of Peace'.

Get into the habit of recognising what is causing you to lose your peace and choose to look to the solution found in Jesus. Paul of the bible tells us to let the peace of Christ rule in our hearts. Taking our eyes off what has hurt us or is wrong but fixing them on what Jesus has done for us. When we let God's love and grace and healing into our hearts, we begin to experience that peace in Christ which overflows to other people in our lives improving our relationships and drawing them closer to Jesus also.

Colossians 3:15 'And let the peace of Christ rule in your hearts, to which indeed you were called in one body. And be thankful'.

Talk to God in prayer about your worries. Worry often leads to anxiety and is the enemy of peace. God invites you to talk to Him and cast your cares on Him, time and time again until you can let them go and leave them with Him.

1 Peter 5:7 'casting all your anxieties on him, because he cares for you'.

Philippians 4:6-7 'do not be anxious about anything, but in everything by prayer and supplication with thanksgiving let your requests be made known to God. And the peace of God, which surpasses all understanding will guard your hearts and your minds in Christ Jesus'.

Living in the knowledge each day that the Holy Spirit lives within you. If you have accepted Jesus as your Lord and Saviour, God gives you the Holy Spirit (Eph 1.13).

Peace is one of the nine fruits of the Holy Spirit.

Galatians 5:22-23 'But the fruit of the Spirit is love, joy, peace, patience, kindness, goodness, faithfulness, gentleness, self-control; against such things there is no law'.

John 14:27 'Peace I leave with you; my peace I give to you. Not as the world gives do I give to you. Let not your hearts be troubled, neither let them be afraid'.

The path to peace is found by putting your faith and trust in God.

Psalm 107:28-29 'Then they cried to the Lord in their trouble, and he delivered them from their distress. He made the storm be still, and the waves of the sea were hushed.

Isaiah 26:3-4 'You keep him in perfect peace whose mind is stayed on you, because he trusts in you. Trust in the Lord for ever, for the Lord God is an everlasting rock'.

Peace is not the absence of chaos but the presence and promises of God.

John 16:33 'I have said these things to you, that in me you may have peace. In the world you will have tribulation. But take heart; I have overcome the world'.

Peace is knowing with full certainty that God is in control.

LIVING IT OUT DAY TO DAY

The Holy Spirit lives within you, recognise that you need to be aware of what is causing you to lose your peace, what is it that you are focusing on or not trusting God with and then turn to Jesus for the solution.

Talk to God about your worries and cast your anxieties on Him in prayer for he cares for you.

Desire to walk with the Holy Spirit daily, write down some ways that you can live this out day to day.

BREATH AWARENESS

Spend 5-10 minutes practising this deep way of breathing. Inhale through your nose, breathe deeply so you can feel your abdomen expand, hold for a few seconds before releasing your breath slowly through your mouth.

Jesus Calms a Storm. Mark 4:35-41

On that day when evening had come, he said to them, "Let us go across to the other side." And leaving the crowd, they took him with them in the boat, just as he was. And other boats were with him. And a great windstorm arose, and the waves were breaking into the boat, so that the boat was already filling. But he was in the stern, asleep on the cushion. And they woke him and said to him, "Teacher, do you not care that we are perishing?" And he awoke and rebuked the wind and said to the sea "Peace! Be still!" And the wind ceased, and there was a great calm. He said to them, "Why are you so afraid? Have you still no faith? And they were filled with great fear and said to one another, "Who then is this, that even the wind and sea obey him?"

BREATH PRAYERS

This is a great short scripture for calming your mind when in a stressful situation or worries are starting to come over you day or night. Bring your focus back to Jesus and the words he spoke to calm the wind and waves.

Mark 4:39 'Peace, be still'.

Breathe in; Peace

Breathe out; Be Still

MEDITATION

The Priestly Blessing

Numbers 6:24-26

'The Lord bless you; the Lord make his face to shine upon you and be gracious to you; the Lord lift up his countenance upon you and give you peace'.

As you meditate upon this blessing from God, make it personal to you.

'The Lord Bless me, the Lord make his face to shine upon me and be gracious to me,

The Lord lift up his countenance upon me and give me peace'.

Amen.

PRAYER

Dear Heavenly Father, in the midst of everything happening in my life and in this world, I ask for your peace to rule in my heart and life. Thank you for making your unwavering peace available to me. Come into every area of my life and be the focus of my mind, heart, and actions. Let me find comfort and rest in your presence, in Jesus' name, Amen.

MINDFULNESS ACTIONS

Continue to journal and write at least three things that you are grateful to God for.

Each day needs to be different to build upon your gratefulness, give thanks to God in prayer.

Practice 5 out of 7 days.

Breath Awareness

Breath Prayers - Mark 4:39

Meditation - Numbers 6: 24-26

Saying grace - At least one meal a day, taking the time to prepare a healthy and nutritious meal/snack. Enjoy with a glass of water, before or afterwards.

Mindful walk or time outside.

Five Senses exercise - Take some time to have 10 minutes to use your five senses.

Start by taking a few slow breaths and ask yourself…

Name three things you can hear?

Notice three things that you can see?

What are three things that you can feel?

Consider three things that you can smell?

Is there anything that you can taste?

Consider the answers to your questions, one sense at a time. Give thanks to God.

SESSION SIX - JOY

Have you considered the difference between happiness and joy?

Some thoughts…

Happiness comes and goes.

Joy runs deep and overflows.

Happiness is fleeting and based on situation and circumstance.

Joy endures hardship and trials, connects with true meaning and purpose.

Happiness doesn't share with other emotions such as sadness.

Joy can share space with other emotions at the same time.

Happiness is an outward expression, reliant on external factors.

Joy is an inner feeling that comes from connection with God.

Many things in life can make us happy; our family, children, work, hobbies, good news, pets and so on. Our friends are also wonderful blessings in our lives. However, happiness is fragile and reliant upon everything going well.

Joy on the other hand is grander than happiness, joy is a fruit of the spirit and available to everyone who connects with God through Jesus his son.

Galatians 5:22-23

'But the fruit of the Spirit is love, joy, peace, patience, kindness, goodness, faithfulness, gentleness, self-control; against such things there is no law'.

Romans 14:17

'For the Kingdom of God is not a matter of eating and drinking but of righteousness and peace and joy in the Holy Spirit'.

We need Joy to have the strength to live the Christian life. God said to Nehemiah in 8:10

'The Joy of the Lord is your strength'. Nehemiah knew true joy and restoration could only come from an inner strength provided by the Lord.

HOW CAN WE KNOW TRUE JOY?

Joy comes when we completely trust and have faith in God in every aspect of our lives.

Joy is the outflow of trust in the one who is fully trustworthy. In Him we have hope in any situation we may face.

Romans 15:13

'May the God of hope fill you with all joy and peace in believing, so that by the power of the Holy Spirit you may abound in hope'.

1 Peter 1:8-9

'Though you have not seen him, you love him. Though you do not see him, you believe in him and rejoice with joy that is inexpressible and filled with glory, obtaining the outcome of your faith, the salvation of your souls'.

We praise God and give Him thanks for He is always good. As we have discovered in previous sessions there is always so much to be grateful for regardless of our current situation or circumstances.

Psalm 107:1

'Oh give thanks to the Lord, for he is good, for his steadfast love endures forever'.

We have a God who loves us more than we can imagine, he is a God who is more powerful than we can comprehend.

1 John 4:9-10

'In this the love of God was made manifest among us, that God sent his only Son into the world, so that we might live through him. In this is love, not that we have loved God but that he loved us and sent his Son to be the propitiation for our sins'.

1 Chronicles 29:11

'Yours, O Lord, is the greatness and the power and the glory, and the victory and the majesty, for all that is in the heavens and in the earth is yours. Yours is the Kingdom, O Lord, and you are exalted as head above all'.

God is never changing; he is the same yesterday, today and forever.

Hebrews 13:8

'Jesus Christ is the same yesterday and today and forever'.

God is forever faithful and his word full of promises to us are true.

2 Corinthians 1:20

'For all the promises of God find their Yes in him. That is why through him we utter our Amen to God for his glory'.

He knows the beginning to the end, and those who love God we can be sure that he is working all things together for our good.

Revelation 1:8

"I am the Alpha and the Omega" says the Lord God, "who is and who was and is to come, the Almighty".

Romans 8:28

'And we know that for those who love God all things work together for good, for those who are called according to his purpose'.

Ultimately God has a rescue plan for all who receive him through His son Jesus, we have the hope of eternal life.

Titus 1:2-3

'In hope of eternal life, which God, who never lies, promised before the ages began and at the proper time manifested in his word through the preaching with which I have entrusted by the command of God our Saviour'.

ACTION

God is Sovereign over all of creation and what we read in scripture teaches us that He can be trusted with all aspects of our lives in life and death. If something matters to us, we can be sure that it matters to God also. He cares about the smallest detail of our lives.

Write down what you are going to begin to trust God with today, then spend some time giving it to Him in prayer.

As we now come to the end of the Eden Well-being course, we come back to the scripture we first read and meditated upon right at the beginning.

The True Vine - Read John 15:1-17

Let us now remind ourselves of how we are to receive Jesus' Joy and live it out day to day.

John 15:4 'Abide in me, and I in you. As the branch cannot bear fruit by itself, unless it abides in the vine, neither can you unless you abide in me'.

John 15:5 'I am the vine; you are the branches. Whoever abides in me and I in him, he is that bears much fruit, for apart from me you can do nothing'.

John 15:9 'As the Father has loved me, so have I loved you. Abide in my love'.

John 15:10 'If you keep my commandments just as I have kept my Fathers commandments and abide in his love'.

John 15:11

'These things I have spoken to you, that my joy may be in you, and that your joy may be full'.

Like we have learnt throughout the course, we don't have to rely on our own efforts to know true joy, we have Jesus' supernatural joy living on the inside of us as we abide in Him.

BREATH AWARENESS

(As precious weeks).

BREATH PRAYERS

Nehemiah 8:10 'For the joy of the Lord is your strength'.

Breathe in: For the joy of the Lord

Breathe out: is your strength.

MEDITATION

John 15:11

'These things I have spoken to you, that my joy may be in you, and that your joy may be full'.

We can make this scripture personal to us as we meditate...

'These things you have spoken to me, that your joy may be in me, and that my joy may be full'.

PRAYER

Dear Heavenly Father,

I thank you that as I place my trust in you, and as I truly abide in you, I can know true Joy. Thank You that you love me more than I could ever possibly imagine, that you are never changing, you are the same yesterday, today and forever and I can build my life upon your truth as a solid foundation. Lord only you know the beginning to the end, and you say those who love you can be sure that you are working all things together for good. Help me to walk closely in step with the Holy Spirit at all times, draw me to desire to know you more by reading your word and praying so that I may become more like your Son Jesus. For it is in Jesus' name I pray, Amen.

MINDFULNESS ACTIONS

Practice 5 out of 7 days.

Breath Awareness

Breath Prayers - Nehemiah 8:10

Meditation - John 15:11

My hope is that you have used the tools you have learnt throughout the wellbeing course. That you will continue to practise breath awareness, breath prayers and meditating on the word of God. I hope that you will revisit this wellbeing course from time to time as a refresher.

God Bless,

Kerry x.

Find me on Facebook 'Eden Well-Being' and Instagram 'edenwell_being'.

ACKNOWLEDGEMENTS

Scripture quotations are from The ESV® Bible (The Holy Bible, English Standard Version®), © 2001 by Crossway, a publishing ministry of Good News Publishers. Used by permission. All rights reserved.

Definition of 'Peace' - Google Dictionary 2023 (Powered by Oxford Languages).